Blue Wanderings
and other poems

by

Teddy Jewell

Copyright©2022 by Teddy Jewell

All world rights reserved

No part of this book may be reproduced, stored in a retrieval system, or transmitted in any form or by any means electronic, mechanical, photocopying, recording or otherwise, without the prior consent of the publisher.

Readers are encouraged to go to www.MissionPointPress.com to contact the author or to find information on how to buy this book in bulk at a discounted rate.

Published by Mission Point Press

2554 Chandler Rd.

Traverse City, MI 49696

(231) 421-9513

www.MissionPointPress.com

ISBN 978-1-958363-15-7

Library of Congress Control Number 2022911337

Printed in the United States of America

*For my mom, Sarah Jewell,
and for
KC, Aleigha, and Alyssa*

Contents

	Page
1	
Return of a New Spring	8
Emerald Ashes	9
Marigold Sun	10
Sun and Moon	11
Mobile Sky	12
What Would I Do, If I Was Certain I Lost You?	13
The Final Reality	14
2	
And the Knots Become Harder to Separate	16
The Addiction of Self Hypnosis	17
I Feel It Knocking	18
Bitter Green Tea	19
Love Is a Talented Ventriloquist	20
Chasing the Sound	21
A Muse in the Greenhouse	22
Safe	23
Marrow	24
Hunger Pains	25
Sorry I Didn't Exist Before	26
If You Left	27
Jungle Birds	28
Limited String	29
Remnant Thief	30
Sky Blue	33
Adulting	34
What Kind of Spectacle Am I?	35
The Storm's Teeth	36
Horizon Falling	37
Precious	38
Grand Piano	39
New Life	

Have I Lived?	40
Organic Identity Manifestation	41
State of Being	42
New Season	43

3

Blue Wanderings	46
Black Ice	47
Who Knew?	48
My Full Attention	49
True Beauty	50
Totem	51
Where Do You Go?	52
Foundation	53
The Air Around Love Wanders	54
Love Language	55
Something Meaningful	56
If Time Had a Shade	57
Lovers' Cocoon	58
An Afterimage of Our Future	59
Fragments (A Delicate Thought)	60
If I Die Before the World	61
Eternal	62
Eternity's End	63

1

Return of a New Spring

I imagine it's quite painful for a flower to bloom
At the return of a new spring.

The flower's habit of dormant sleep
Must be destroyed
For it to unfold and inhale the sunlight.

The winter that forced upon its frozen roots
No longer persuades the living
To seek refuge into themselves
And turn away from the outside world.

The blooming sky
Forces their absence out of place
And beckons for Earth to do the same.

The flower, recalling its true strength
Forces its old life to evolve
And expand as it finally reflects
The glow of its ancient mentor.

Emerald Ashes

You're just as beautiful as they were
How they glowed
simmering the air
offering a warm solace

Emerald ashes coated the trees
in a layer of comfortable danger
and risk

But I'd give anything to watch again
As the heated green dress falls
beneath your hips
moments before lighting the forest

Marigold Sun

Watered-down marigolds
Thrown against the waning moon
To make up for what was missing

Drunk on pleasure
Or was it pain
      He knew both would grant their own sting

The golden sun bought a bouquet a day
      On her march across the sky
And she left a piece of her behind
      To keep the flowers alive

Their petals remained open
Until after the moon finished his nightly routine
And sent him the sun they held within
Delivering her love letter in the moon's bloom

Sun and Moon

I know that if we strip ourselves
of our weighted, earthly fabric
we will become astronauts

and everyone will watch
as we drift throughout eternity
and access the life
we've always felt belonged to us

We'll stay tethered together
We are the space crew
who discovers the life no one has seen
And we'll hold it between our orbit

with our hands clasped
like the sun and moon

Mobile Sky

What moves you each second of the day?
Your clouds crawl across my line of sight,
then vanish.

Astrologers say it's our planet's own doing.
A game our atmosphere plays on the clouds.

But what if something neighboring
our realm of understanding
is causing this whirring of winds?

A being of similar features,
past flaws, and learning,
carrying the sky around.

Were we to grow bigger
than the planet itself,
we'd know all the more
And probably too soon.

Out of the picture as that may be,
to dream of something uniquely fitting
that could be your truth.

What Would I Do, If I Was Certain I Lost You?

I honestly don't know
Somewhere in my head
I've tried to let it go

There's an image
like a diamond formed
under the pressure of what you and I could've been
and I despise it
Really

It places a hollow weight in the back of my mind
as I pointlessly avoid missteps
I can't afford

If I make the wrong choice in hesitation or overreaction
I could lose you forever
and maybe I am closer to that point than I'd like

The image itself lies
as a glimpse at something far better than
our present placement

At the end of it all
I truly hope for you to be the one
who lets me know I can rest peacefully
I'll have learned to value my mistakes as lessons
and not missed chances
to avoid regret

The Final Reality

What if the stars were suspended raindrops?
What if every raindrop were a distant planet
Falling out of orbit
To its final resting place?

What if our Earth is the final reality,
And we're converting it into disposable goods?
Are our landfills and dumpsters just nature's toy boxes,
Similar to the oceans and forests?

Everything ends up somewhere,
A collection of ancient somethings.
Nowhere must be a place on Earth.

2

And the Knots Become Harder to Separate

Subconscious visitor

I fall prey to your false imagery
but grasp at the beautiful threads
like the sandmen instruct

Each thread weighs a lifetime on my mind
and constricts my heart

All of it is wrong
Reality visits no one while they sleep

And still, I drag the dark thread
adding it to my amassing ball of string
The lines tangle themselves
accepting the intruder as their own

And I am left with blurred dreams
and knotted memories
The knots harder to separate

The Addiction of Self Hypnosis

There's an addict
        but not one with an addiction to alcohol
                The habit grew from a toxic poison
        derived from a beautifully frightening flower
the ego

In small doses
        negative symptoms are negligible
                They can push forward in confidence
        and create comfortable environs around themselves

In large doses
        the flower's extract can turn someone
                numb to the outside world
        There is only the addict and pain

Their faults hide from their eyes
        their mind reshapes the world
                to match what they believe is an inner reality
the truth

They can't see distortion
        They lose track of their manipulation
                And the ego flower blooms again
        offering more to consume

The addict accepts
        they feel like the rest of the world
                offers only isolation
        And they enjoy temporary warmth
                not the warmth of true connection

Like someone who's been badly burned
        because the world got too hot
                Instead of finding a warm spot
        away from dangerous zones
                they idolize a false fire
a blooming flower
        that blinds the addict
to their own pain

I Feel It Knocking

I feel it knocking
as if I'm the door
I've picked up stomping
in a subtle effort to ignore

the maladies of life
I've come to adore
Though I've thrown away my pen
and made it harder to record

a voice on the other side
won't let me have peace
unless I scribble a page
and tear out a new piece

I've slid a dark letter
scratched in black ink
that stops the shouts and knocking
but only for a week

On the inside, I can find distractions
keeping me busier than before
but I can always feel it knocking
as if I'm the door

The more I avoid it
the more interesting the other side grows
Sometimes it's hard to want to ruin it
because excitement never really knows

The stomping gets old
to my partner and I
By now the apartment's shaking
and I can only guess why

until I write a new page
before the day that I die
For I am the door
and the people on either side

And if the reunion keeps stopping
I will always feel it knocking

Bitter Green Tea

Remember, bitter green tea
Remember the thought of you and me
Coat my throat with a little caffeine
Coat my mind with memories so serene

Remember the time, wish we had eternity
Remember the day we learned our melody
Coat our bodies in wrinkles, our life in memory
Coat my voice in rough silk as I cry an apology

Remember what I did—it was only partially me
Remember what happened when we had to leave
Coat the table in warped rings
Coat your body with a coat

We left before our time was up
Before the tea was ever cold

Love Is a Talented Ventriloquist

who has mastered the art
of throwing their voice

A voice that can seduce the audience
into fits of passion
opposite the destination of its original source

The sound of love's echo is enough
to capture the heart of another
But no true companion may be near

Love sounds good enough to those
who only live by their ears
and are comfortable
absorbing misdirection

Chasing the Sound

I heard something early in the morning
        when I wasn't listening
It always catches me off guard

        You've twisted our code
        but it still feels like you
        I stopped listening
        but caught the end
of your latest transmission

        of what I grasped and understood
        It was the tone that trailed after your words
        running through the hair on my arms

It grazed every disc in my spine

        The morning stayed quiet

I'm back to chasing sounds
        Next time I'll be ready to catch them
        if the words come back around

A Muse in the Greenhouse

And the hose was left running in the garden.
Your hands become pale
as you make sense of the weeds
darting up the side of your gentle home.

A muse in the greenhouse,
but tending to the weeds comes first.
What wilts is what's left unfinished and neglected—
a stained glass dream, a window holding back tears.

She sits in the greenhouse, afraid to walk to her garden
and bury weeds. Stems and roots grab at her forearm,
the thorns leaving behind scars.
A muse in the greenhouse sits. The plants beside her wilt.

Safe

The challenge is finding someone who feels like home,
    who opens the door with ever-expanding arms
when real homes don't always offer the same welcome.

    You've been roaming the woods for many lifetimes
and never found shelter in the wilderness you've searched.
    But when those eyes are met with an accepting gaze
the wild can be tamed.

    When you've grown tired of fighting every unknown,
a bed waits for your warm spirit
    to rest your weary muscles and strained eyes.

The ones who fend for themselves
    and square off with fate
meet the one challenge they can't shake:

    Finding the one who tends to their pains and aches
and offers a home where they feel safe.

Marrow

Break my
legs
Please
I no longer want to walk alone

Take my hands
I carry
weight greater than I
asked for

Remove
my jaw
silenced before
I no longer have anything to say

But that's not
going to help
I want
everything back

Like blood
in my veins
And marrow in
my bones
I'll get to where
I need
to go

There
they'll hear
me
Work with me
walk
with me

Hunger Pains

I starved my soul again
for human connection
Love is powerful
but can guide you in the wrong direction

Love remains
But these soul-bound hunger pains
won't dissipate

Love is not the only thing I was put here to make
I'm the unknown captor of my own identity
And I to myself am
estranged

Help me destroy this distance so
even I can't put myself away

Sorry I Didn't Exist Before

I did it in my unknowing attempt at self-defense
But most of all
I'm sorry you didn't stick around
To learn, to watch me take form

The world is a disastrous place
It drove me into silence
It stifled my interests
Left me stranded in the middle of nowhere

The world stole my voice
Like being dropped in the middle of an unknown land
No one could understand me, nor I them

So I became quiet
Learned how everyone spoke
And found over time, I could match their speech

Not my own words, but at least
I could follow what everyone thought
But the world continued to fight back

In my ability to echo everyone
I lost myself

My heart, taken away
I, everything, had never felt so pointless

I stopped feeling
I didn't mind

If You Left

Everyone I care about
Is contemplating what
The world would look
Like if they left it

I'd go blind
Nothing could
Bring back my sight
Not even the
World's best surgeons

I'd choose not to
Perceive a world where
They were gone

Seems weak
Not to accept reality
But if reality took
My only reasons for
Being involved in the
Influence of life,
My interactions with
The world would
Diminish

Jungle Birds

Jungle birds eat insects
like I eat my feelings
over and over
leg after leg

They crawl down my throat
while I choke and struggle
to keep them from climbing back up

Tonight the birds sing
I watch carefully
waiting for the insects
to return to the open

Instead, I hear
the tones of their past lives
coating their voices
in melody

A harmony of acceptance
and release of what's inside
        without losing what's needed to survive

Limited String

String them together,
words that will be used against me.

String them
together until the flow of their sounds
drifts forward with ease.

I, listening to words left unsaid
will tie on silences of my own.
One after another, absences
of mention, twisted, knotted
on limited string.

Remnant Thief

I'll make use of what
they all leave behind
Remnants of translated feelings

While many remain in their heads' penthouses
consuming the easy bits,
the tasty facts,
the delicious analysis

I'll remain in the body's core
collecting the gold dust of the unspoken
off the heart's floor

Sky Blue

Back to Red for a brief time
my favorite color when I was young
in sharp disobedience to my mother. Her favorite
color on me: Blue

> It brings out my eyes and makes them pop
> I'm grateful for you
> who always looked me in the eyes
Maybe a Blue shirt helped you see my heart too

Maybe the color
like Red for bulls
pulled my true feelings out
from deep below

> They ran down my face
> caught by the sky-colored fabric
> As I get older, I'm realizing
> the magic to your motherhood

I'm sorry
I chose to block it with Red
My independence leaked out through my pupils
and changed the color of everything

> Blue: Green
> Emotion: envy
> Passion: Red
> my bullseye

Red like the lights
atop police cars that pulled me over
for moving too fast

> Red like the Camaro I drove to school
> hoping to impress my friends
> who were born wearing Red

I was growing and learning faster than before
But my emotions were frozen
hibernating
No Blue to stir them awake

    You never told me but I'm sure you knew
    that it wasn't just my eyes that popped in Blue
    I still get stuck wearing Red
    but Blue helps me connect with
the parts of me that come from you

Over time I've watched my eyes develop Purple petals
I know you'll love those
Like a growing field of flowers
they'll always have a color planted by you

Sky Blue

Adulting

But we can't act like children anymore.
Adulthood should represent bravery,
Where fear may still set in
But we're no longer able to hide from it,

Shutting down will turn us into unmoving sharks,
A living dead ready to chomp
Only on the food that swims close enough.
We have to learn to move,

Keep the dancing spirit of a child,
The unbreakable bones
And relentless energy.
But leave the paradoxical need to play hide-n-seek,
Feeding off the spotlight at the same time.

We're adults in humanity's spotlight,
We don't need to be front row.
Age is the wisest teacher.
It'll tell you to stay young at heart
But learn humility and forgiveness,
Independence and passion along the way.

What Kind of Spectacle Am I?

I need to fall in love with my personal growth.
Who am I when I'm the only voice filling the room?

Who am I when it's just my judgment I can fall prey to?
I've been scared of myself.

I'm not a villain who needs restraints to construct a lifestyle.
Empty is using another's dictionary to translate my story.

With the broken lenses removed,
What kind of spectacle am I?

I am the farmer tending to growth and planting in preparation
For a great harvest in the sky.

In figuring out life, I might stumble like a newborn
Taking in the world for the first time.

I have to forgive but not forget my mistakes because
They are my teachers.

In accepting the difficult parts of my life and gratitude
For my journey, my life is starting to bloom.

Every second that passes is a wiser me.
I can exist not in paradox, but in creation.
I'm learning to love every iteration.

The Storm's Teeth

Not only does a storm have eyes,
you can feel its teeth sink in
while you wait for the tension to release.

The other side of pain
is covered in fog and harsh winds,
and the ground you're standing on is too distorted
to see. Your instincts now too contorted
to believe what you already know,
yet your grip hasn't slipped and your strength
provides shelter.

You can outlast the rain.

Horizon Falling

There isn't a lot within our control
        It's like a state of constant falling

Eventually, we find a horizon
        falling within us

We decide we can exist within the descent
        Living an entire lifetime

enjoying the well of consciousness
        created by everyone, including ourselves

Precious

Don't pretend like we're perfect.
I couldn't pretend to be something so fragile.
Perfect only lasts before the first mistake,
and mistakes are guaranteed.

Glass drops and then shatters,
but if we look at what gets rebuilt
as something more precious,
then I exist within the cracks,
and we'll make it more beautiful.

Grand Piano

We're playing as we go
A flow of random interactions
Our decisions are like the hum of a grand piano
And the great Composer allows us

His melodic keys
To push ourselves up and down
Communicating at our own pace
Decoding each other's sound

While adding and reacting
Conversing like the greatest jazz players
Whose brass lined the warm sound
With a shimmer of positive and negative tones
In a song, eternal and improvisational

New Life

I can feel it,
the itch to let my mind speak.
Too often I get wrapped up in obnoxious
intruding noises
that cause my voice to remain silent.

If the world was like a newborn child,
too often I'd feel like a parental figure.
It knows nothing of the life I want,
but I know too much of what it thinks it needs.

And if I know what the child needs
at every scream and screech,
my thoughts and feelings aren't one of them
so they quiet and disappear.

I am a part of this new life,
like the generational DNA within me.
So my voice isn't meant to stand alone.
My cries are the world's cries, my life
is a piece of yours.

I need to care for myself and the world equally
and remain the caretaker of my identity.
Distractions are my fault when
I let them erase me.

I Have Lived

You have to hold onto the belief
that you're something the world says you're not.
Their goal is to marginalize and condense,

try to convince you to live the life
that those before and around you
have lived.
Have you lived?

Have you felt yourself align
with a purpose undying?

You know who you are.
Don't let something that's never been inside your heart
pretend that it can piece you apart
and determine who you are.

Your first job:
Find it yourself.
Second job:
Close your fists and don't let the world take it away.

Organic Identity Manifestation

I am who I currently am
But I have to think it through.

I still exist alone,
But the story behind my existence
And the lessons I've learned
Make for a compelling character.
I need to see where life takes him.

This is my organic manifestation of identity.
This is me as me,
And not only me.

I am bigger than my materialization,
But life likes to sprinkle
Forgetfulness over my head.

My self-realization is the buffer,
But I must contemplate on it
So as not to let it decay.

State of Being

Like shooting marbles
By kicking rocks
My path is less defined
Than I originally thought

It's good
I'm glad
I never wanted to fixate
On the journey I had

I want to see the full scope of life
Accept what comes my way
I won't hold the rope
And march through fate

For the rope is an illusion
The events that compose my life
Are just one state
Of being

New Season

There's this feeling of breaking
It feels like I'm breathing

In the gust of a new season
When everything starts to change

When the leaves lose the appendages
That fused them to their tree

And the distance between tree and ground
Changes the leaf's perception of everything

3

Blue Wanderings

Like camouflaged birds
      against a sky

      batted by stormy weather
the wanderings
           wonder how it feels
      to kiss the sun

To love the sun
      is not as warm as they think
          It can't follow them
      into the next day

can't follow them beneath
      the rain-filled clouds

Blue wanderings shivering
          blue until the sun returns
      a muse for them to sing to

Black Ice

Low traction, wheels
Biting into loose snow
Full speed, nothing to hold

If true love is the time to let go
Let it be
black ice, a winter road

Drivers out of control
Learning to love letting go

Who Knew?

This story of ours
is one I can't predict.
I, its only writer
until now. I thought I only needed love.
Instead, it was the vehicle that brought me to the fire.

My reflection on the flames
was a stranger with my face,
same heart, but darker,
same soul, but worn from struggle.

Through the flickering light
I could see you in your own battle.

Who knew we'd win the fight we never chose to enter?
Who knew we'd already be hungry for more?

My Full Attention

They await the moment
I give them my full attention
Though I will have been doing so
Since the last time we spoke

They sit in my mind
Bathed in the light that flows
Over the shape of their figure

Now here I am
Awaiting the moment
They welcome me inside
Ask me to shut the blinds

True Beauty

Can we ever fully understand
something we find truly beautiful,
or will we always be fascinated by the unknown
and the potential to learn more?

Do you think I'm beautiful?

I pray attraction is a two-way street
that leads us closer to each other
and takes us further from the other's horizon.

The closer we get,
the more light shines on who we truly are,
the more beautiful you grow.

Understanding is more fascinating
than the mystery.
Understanding is how I know
for sure that you are something beautiful.

Totem

The flutter of those delicate eyelashes
and the presence of a finely tuned smile
are enough to sway the butterflies
to envy and convince the world
of your own necessity.

The birds walk away from their morning songs
accepting second place to your voice.
And the flowers forget their colors,
astonished by your skin's ethereal glow.

They'd all choose to be you
if they had the choice.

But to the weary
and those who've never known their own beauty,
you stand as a totem.
One day,
they will come into their own.

Where Do You Go?

When your eyes glaze over
Are you free from yourself
While you're there
Something that takes

You so far away
Can't be as free as you think
And you could get lost forever in
An empty stare

So clever
To be able to sink
Into a pseudo-reality
And not care

Make sure you don't ever
Lose the key
Much less hide it from me
It wouldn't be fair

Foundation

These walls have never felt so unstable.
The frame is off-balance.
The house's joints creak
under the stress.

It's a principle of thought and decision.

Can't you see the cracks
hidden in our foundation?

It must be nice to believe
these walls could never fall.

I've seen the house shake and shudder
with your fear.
I know I can't stay here.

The wall crumbles, growing
piles of rubble in the corners.
My fear has started cracking me,

but I'm rebuilding my foundation.
I can tell you're seeing it.

The Air Around Love Wanders

in through my window
snuffing out candles.
Some good,
some bad
comfort.

It freshens my senses
dulls out the pain.
Some good, some bad
days.

The air around love wanders,
and some days I'm not sure it's here
Some good,
some bad
uncertainty.

It fills my lungs, cushions my bones,
and I barely feel myself.
Some good.
Some acceptance. Painful.

Love Language

To witness your tongue
Dancing to new choreography.
New sounds emanating from the pressure
Against your teeth and cheek.

Like the echo of a lonely cave-dweller
Singing for a connection
That started:
What's your name?
And ends:
How can I make you happy?

Something Meaningful

Marriage with you
seems frighteningly beautiful
But sometimes I'm frightened
by more than the spectacle

My heart strains at the thought
of you and I
struggling to find meaning in life

We should be more than
a random combination of two
We should be the sum total
of all our favorite parts

     A new identity
built from fully realized selves
Then two halves can make a union
one that deserves a celebration

If Time Had a Shade

it'd be indistinguishable
from the pitch-black
you only get late,
late at night.

As the hours pass
and you're far away
every part of me is dormant.
Void. One.
Empty. Two.
Black. Three.

Seconds become dreams.
Seconds create nightmares
late at night.
Time itself is negative without any light,

a countdown or reminder
of an absence.
The clock mourns the sun's disappearance
at night.

Lovers' Cocoon

A lovers' cocoon
Is a combination in solace
As souls worth their own experiences
Share one together,
Or many if the organic nature
Of the shelter is built
To last.

Under the covers,
Laced in each other's
Arms and legs,
A lovers' cocoon
Reshapes our paradigm,
Commits this point in time
To fusion.

Interlocked memories that blueprint
Our shared influence,
Identically new
And one step towards
Understanding ourselves
A tiny amount more.

An Afterimage of Our Future

Laughter, beautiful
And an afterimage of you and I
Burned into the night sky

Like the screen from an old cinema showing
The reel, woven around our locked fingers
Our lips, framed, our tongues, undressing

God,
You looked so amazing in that dress

Some story
But we could just experience it for ourselves
An afterimage of our future
Shared nights like this

Fragments (A Delicate Thought)

                                                        May 19, 2020
I spent my time away, counting eternity
On each and every one of my fingertips

                                          January 30, 2020
I don't want to be counting the days while I'm here
But I have to count the days I'm gone

                                            April 23, 2020
Distraction, my only muse

                                         February 5, 2020
Somehow I've hidden myself from me
I've found it in you

                                            March 13, 2020
I can't be lost
      in losing myself again

If I Die Before the World
bury me beneath the forbidden stars
so I can see the unknown lands.

I'll join the forces of infinite travelers
who set sail well before my time,
and freely view the universe
as should've been my right before.

I'll discover new worlds,
untouched by the tangible,
only seen through a telescope,
as I capture their likenesses.

Were it too much for my mortal
mind to comprehend,
my spirit will hold
the secrets of adventure and discovery.

I'll join the surrounding matter, send my desire
back to Earth for someone to catch hold.

Eternal

Without a destination
Is there ever an end
To us?

Where would we stop,
Knowing that to finish now
Would make the thing
Incomplete?

Incompletion, it seems,
Is a constant.
So too then,
Is an end.

Eternity's End

Eternity is a much longer road
To travel when you're alone,
And you passed by me,
Long before I found its path.

I still see the signs of your touch
And the flowers that have bloomed
In the sun you've planted.
I never stopped following the remnants.

Ahead of the horizon,
You never slow
And I am forever unable to match
Your pace.

What am I to do then?
How can I reach you,
Eternity's end?

Wait for me.
I'll speak it into existence if I have to.
Wait for me, so we
Can find the thing everyone searches for.

Without fail, we will
No longer feel like we're fighting
To discover it.

We will reach the end.
We will be content.

Acknowledgments

I strongly believe that life cannot exist without the influence of others, and there are many who have influenced me and guided me to the point where I am now publishing a collection like this.

      Firstly, I'd like to thank the publishing team at Mission Point Press: Doug, Tanya, and Sarah for walking me through my first publishing process. Without their guidance and support, this collection wouldn't be here. I'd like to thank both of my sisters for always listening to what I had to say and validating my feelings, even though growing up with me also meant being annoyed by my hyper energy and wondering mind.

I'm truly grateful for my mom. She has taught me nearly everything I know about being a good person. She gave me my heart, both figuratively and literally.

To my partner, KC, who holds my heart, I owe so much love, appreciation, and respect. They have decided to stay by my side during my twenties, when I still have a lot left to figure out. They have been incredibly helpful in my journey of self-healing and self-discovery too.

I'm grateful for everyone on the team at Michigan Creative. Brian, the CEO of MC, helped me connect with Mission Point Press, and the rest of the team has become my creative family.

It's important that I also acknowledge the extensive influence my friends have had on my growth. Connor, Ben, Mitch, Matthew and Mike, thank you for being my brothers. There are many others I'd like to thank too. Anyone who I have ever known, know that you have taken a part in molding who I am, and thus you have taken a part in the words that fill these pages. I have also grown from my interactions with my teachers; everyone has taught me something.

Lastly, I'd like to thank the authors I have read who have reignited and stoked the fire in me to write more, to write in my own unique voice, and to write what I feel as I learn and grow in life. Ray Bradbury; Lou Beach; Karen Russell; Ted Chiang; Molly Mendoza; Ken Liu; Rick Hanson; Richard Mendius, MD; Ram Dass; Leonard Cohen; Tim Freke; Ocean Vuong; Yuval Noah Harari; Keith R. Leonard; Melody Beattie; Don Miguel Ruiz; and Aldous Huxley, thank you for allowing your voices to exist within my mind. I truly value the lessons and conversations we have had.

www.ingramcontent.com/pod-product-compliance
Lightning Source LLC
Chambersburg PA
CBHW052101280426
43673CB00071B/36